1
easy munch

not so easy
2

3
little harder

4

Rolf Heimann's
MIND
munchers

SOUTHWOOD
B O O K S

Southwood Books Limited

3–5 Islington High Street

London N1 9LQ

First published in Australia by Roland Harvey Books, 1998

This edition published in the UK under licence from

Penguin Books Australia Ltd by Southwood Books Limited, 2002

ISBN 1 903207 82 7

Copyright © Rolf Heimann, 1998

Designed by Carlie O'Brien

A CIP catalogue record for this book is available from the British Library

Printed in China by Everbest Printing Co. Ltd

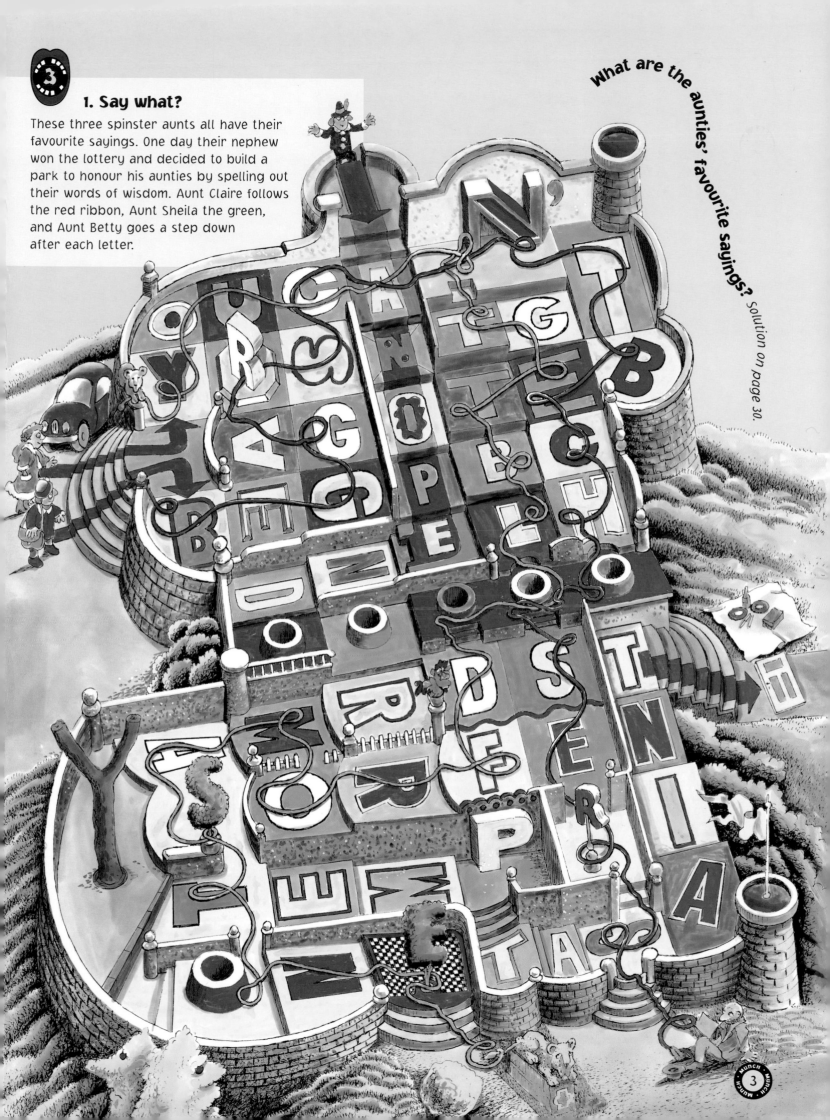

1. Say what?

These three spinster aunts all have their favourite sayings. One day their nephew won the lottery and decided to build a park to honour his aunties by spelling out their words of wisdom. Aunt Claire follows the red ribbon, Aunt Sheila the green, and Aunt Betty goes a step down after each letter.

What are the aunties' favourite sayings? Solution on page 30.

1

2. Sea of surprises

The world is full of life.
If you look carefully, you
can read a message in
this picture.
Solution on page 30.

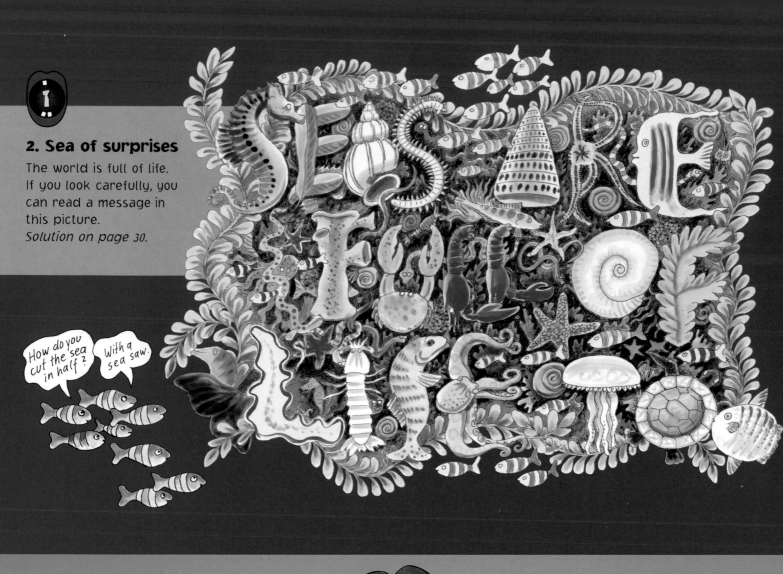

2

3. Tortuous turtle

Turtles are said to be slow,
so don't worry if it takes
you a long time to get
through this maze!

4

4. Pick the pair

Look for the objects needed by the figures below, then find the attached letters and put them into the corresponding spaces! For example, the monkey's pair is the banana, which is attached to the letter 'T'. *Solution on page 30.*

5. Treacherous temple

This is the temple where once upon a time the faithful sought guidance from Saint Camouflage, the patron saint of people who have things to hide. Fourteen eggs are hidden in the grounds, and those who find them, as well as making their way from the red to the blue flag, are all given praise. *Solution on page 30.*

6. Letter litter

Put these letters in the right order. Make sure the pieces fit snugly! *Solution on page 30.*

7. Anna Gram Enterprises

There is no admittance to the premises of Anna Gram Enterprises. "But why?" wondered Carl. "I think we can find out," said Professor X. "Look, somebody has given us a hint by numbering the letters!" *Solution on page 30.*

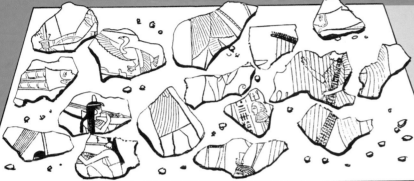

8. Fragments from the Pharaohs

Archaeologists have long been searching for the fragments of a certain ancient Egyptian work of art. Did they find the right ones this time? A total of nine pieces belong in the picture above, but five don't. *Solution on page 30.*

9. Forbidden colours

King Nebuchadnezzar's sculptors managed to produce four identical wise men, but one of the painters made a mistake when it came to colouring them. Which of the figures is different and how many mistakes were made? *Answer on page 30.*

Batman & Robin

...were two legendary giants who were captured by the Trojans and made to serve as guardians of a palace in London. In 1708 their statues were erected at the Guildhall in London.

the WRIGHT BROS.

...started as comedy characters in American silent movies, getting into one fine mess after another. One was fat, the other skinny.

Their permanent enemy is "The Joker". But he has no hope of outsmarting these famous fighters for righteousness. They were created in 1939 by Bob Kane as an answer to "Superman".

Tom Sawyer & Huckleberry Finn

Jack & Jill

...were brother and sister in a fairy-tale. Lost in the woods, they were lured into a gingerbread house by a witch. But the children outsmarted her!

BONNIE & CLYDE

Christians believe that these were the first humans created by God. After eating forbidden fruit, they were chased from paradise.

Hänsel & Gretel

...were created by William Shakespeare. Despite a feud between their parents, they fell in love, and committed suicide rather than stay apart.

ROMULUS & REMUS

One of them was famous as a fighter for truth, justice, freedom and the American way, and the other followed his exploits for the newspaper, *Daily Planet*.

11. Four-star puzzle

Can you trace along the white section of the stars in a single line without lifting your pen from the paper? It can be done, you know!
Solution on page 30.

12. The waiting game

These men have given up trying to get out. Can you help them?

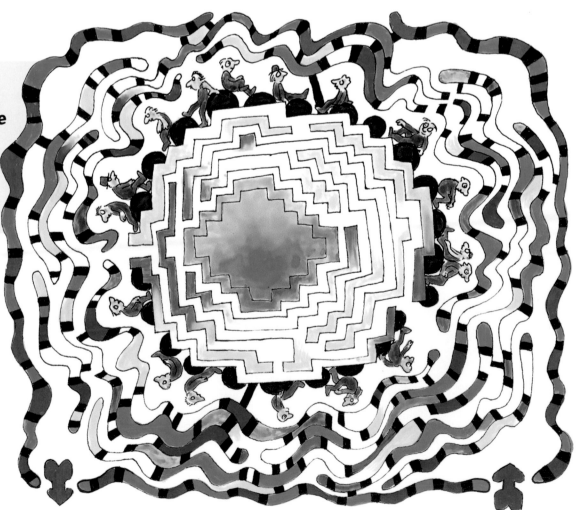

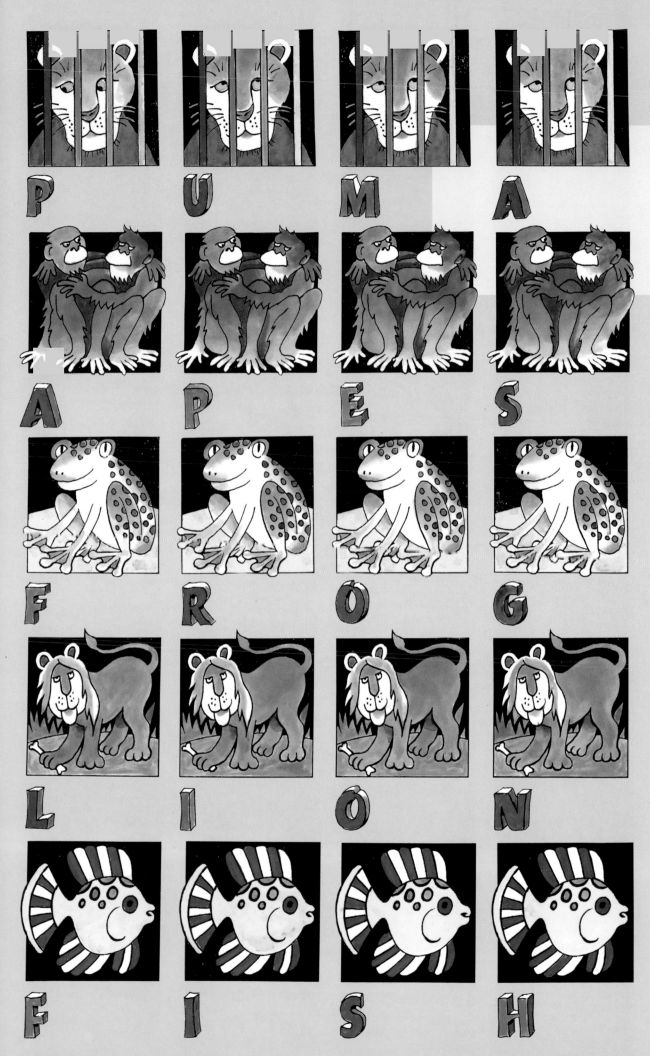

At first glance the rows of pictures may look the same. Find those pictures which are different in some way.

Then use the letters below them to spell out the name of the city. *Solution on page 30.*

P U M A

A P E S

F R O G

L I O N

F I S H

14. Step by step

Step from A to Z through the entire alphabet. Start on A, then move to the bell, then to the cloud.

You have to find the rest of the way by yourself. Solution on page 30.

15. Magic word

Find a magic word by collecting all the letters that bear the secret stamp.
Solution on page 30.

This is the secret stamp.

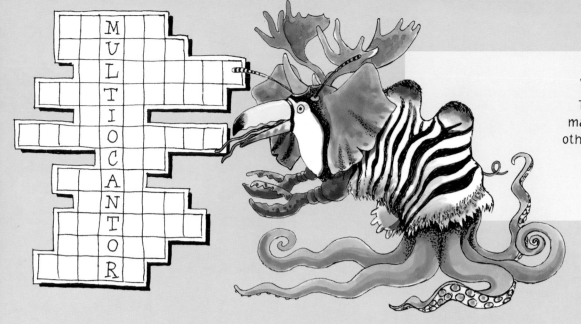

16. What beast is that?

The legendary multiocantor is made up of no less than twelve other animals. Find them all and put their names horizontally into the empty fields.
Solution on page 30.

17. Disk dilemma

When these nine discs are arranged in the right order, the completed stack will display an image. They are keyed to be stacked in one way only. Start from the top or bottom.
Solution on page 31.

18. Age by age

How old are these children? You can work it out by studying their clues.
Solution on page 31.

DORA	
BECKA	
TIM	
ROVER	
RUBY	
KARL	
TINA	

19. Snail trail

Try to get from one side of the forest to the other.

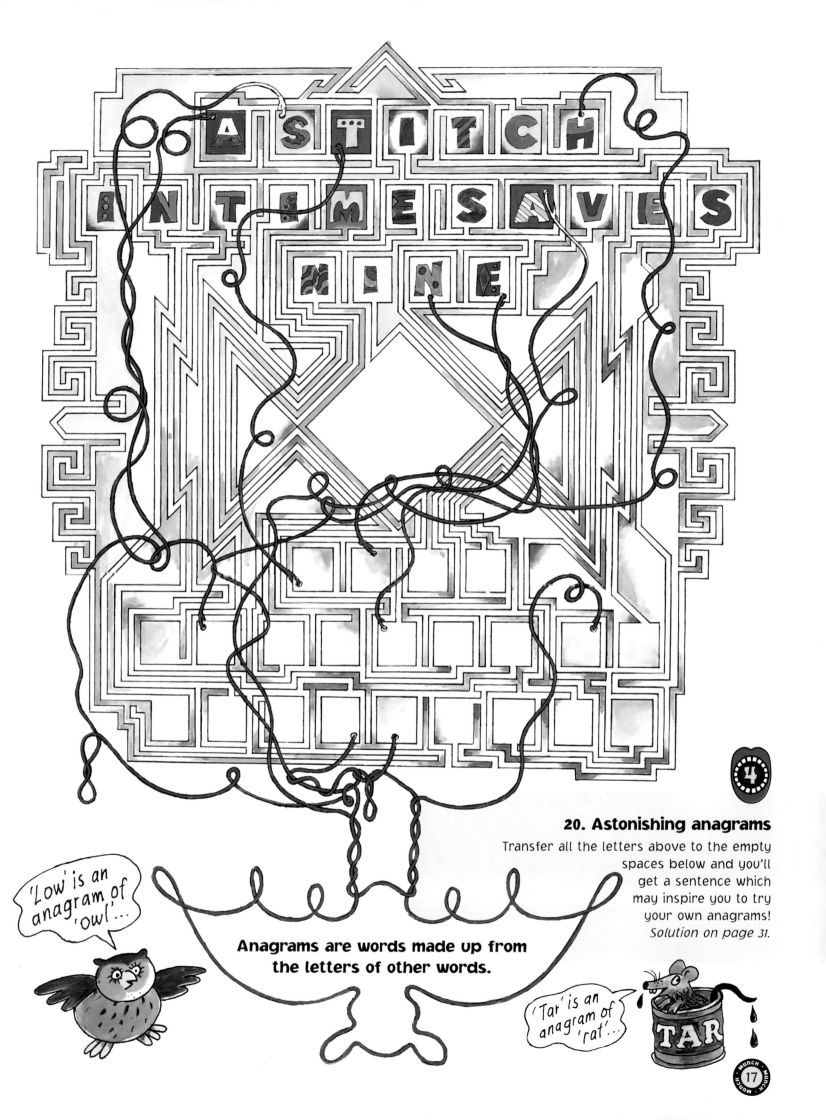

20. Astonishing anagrams

Transfer all the letters above to the empty spaces below and you'll get a sentence which may inspire you to try your own anagrams!
Solution on page 31.

Anagrams are words made up from the letters of other words.

'Low' is an anagram of 'owl'...

'Tar' is an anagram of 'rat'...

21. Opposites attract

The world is full of opposites. Would you believe that this picture contains over forty? Below are some of the more difficult examples. There are more obvious ones which you may find yourself, and they are listed on page 31.

Big – small	light – heavy
thick – thin	male – female
old – new	rich – poor
sad – happy	sunny – rainy
bald – hairy	hungry – sated
strong – weak	broken – whole
sick – healthy	free – caged
colourful – drab	soft – hard
sharp – blunt	cowardly – brave
ugly – pretty	dark – bright
open – closed	naked – dressed
behind – in front	natural – artificial
fierce – gentle	cruel – kind
solid – rickety	crowded – deserted

What's the opposite of 'sulphur-crested'?

22. Restore the story

Before a film or television commercial is shot, it is customary to draw storyboards, which help to plan camera angles, lighting, props etc. Sometimes these drawings are done on loose cards which can be moved around. The storyboard cards below have become mixed up, so that the story-line has been lost altogether. Can you put them into the right order? If you are successful, the letters will spell out the name of the film. *Solution on page 31.*

23. Pegs galore

Square pegs don't fit into round holes! The top and bottom rows have already been clicked together. You'll have to work out yourself how the other pieces fit together. Transfer the lines onto the squares of the grid. *Solution on page 31.*

Lower away!

This is how the pieces fit together...

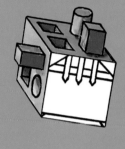

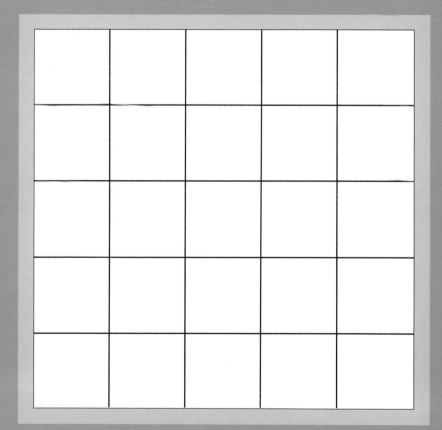

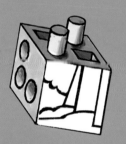

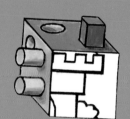

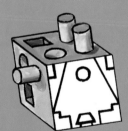

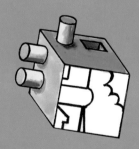

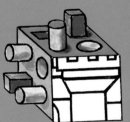

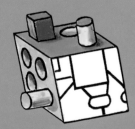

24. Where to?

There's been a malfunction in the airport departure signs: all the letters have been mixed up. If you're smart you can still make sense of them!

Solution on *page 31.*

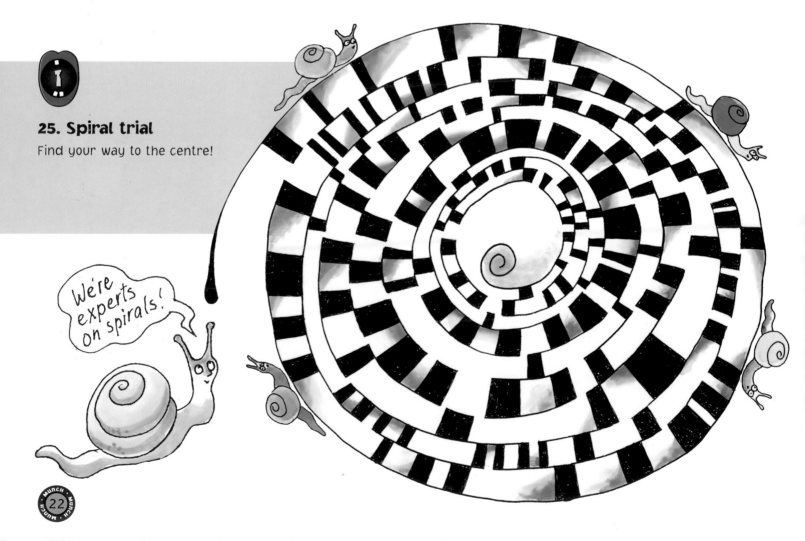

25. Spiral trial

Find your way to the centre!

26. Slot in the slabs

Only one of the blue-sided slabs below fits correctly onto one of the red-sided ones above to make up the design pictured left.

Solution on page 31.

27. Hexed paths

There are eleven ways to make your way through these
hexagons, from left to right. Step only through those hexagons
whose pictures have something in common. Starting from the top

one, for instance, go only through hexagons with a red background. The second? Use only pictures of pigs. The third path: only fish, the fourth: only animals that look backwards. Then? Try to find other ways! *Solution on page 31.*

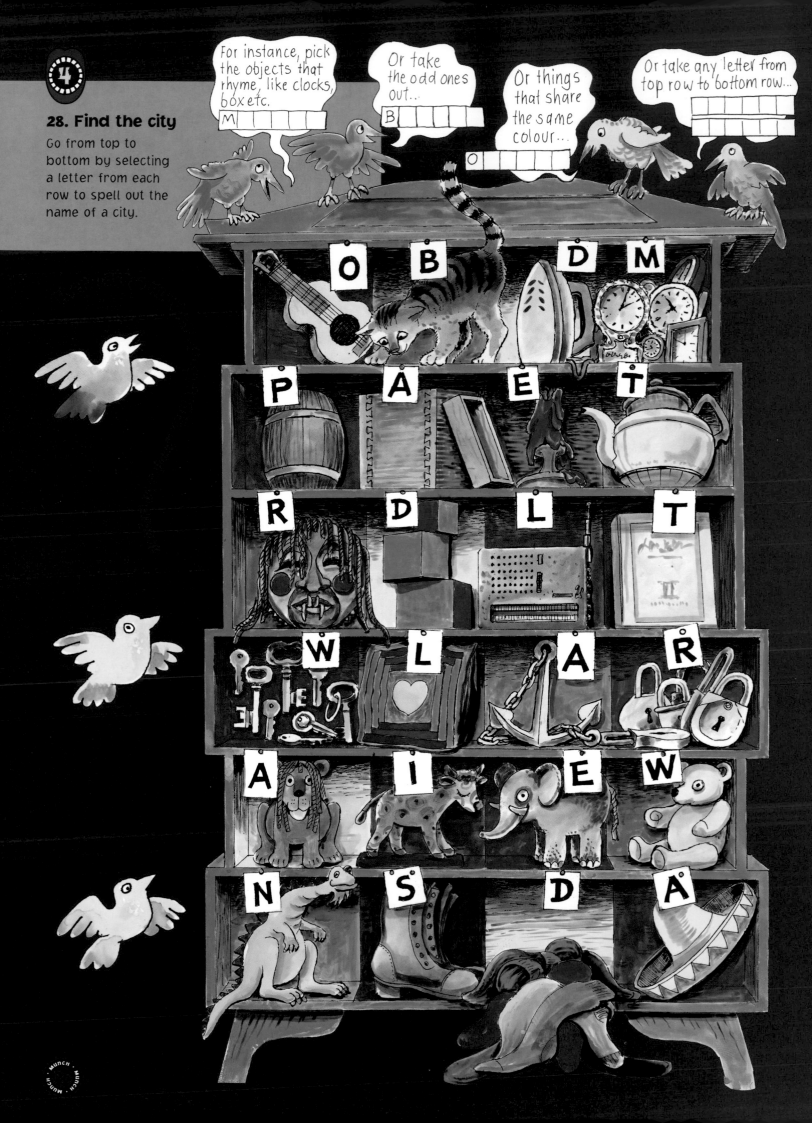

29. Baffling balls

At first sight Chico the juggler's balls may all look the same, but two are different.

Solution on page 31.

30. Mug shots

The police are looking for a mystery woman who has been involved in industrial espionage. Luckily they already know a number of things about her.

She has blue eyes, she wears earrings, she has red hair... It shouldn't be too hard to identify her!

Solution on page 31.

31. Maths mystery

Elisa made a mistake on the first day of her new job! She had to write down numbers given to her on the phone, but when it came to adding them up, she didn't know whether the paper was the right way up. However, her boss looked at it for a minute and said, "Don't worry, just add it up and be done with it!" Why did he say such a thing? *Solution on page 31.*

918
816
886
988

32. Pick up sticks

Which of the sticks was thrown down first and which ones after it? Arrange the letters accordingly and find the name of a famous person.
Solution on page 31.

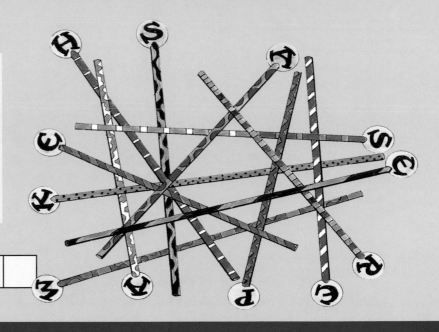

33. Flower power

The bees need to get to the centre of the flower. How will they do it?

What goes 'zzub zzub'?

A bee flying backwards.

Solutions

1. Say what?
The aunts' favourite sayings are:
Aunt Sheila: **"Beggars can't be choosers"**
Aunt Claire: **"You can't get blood from a stone"**
Aunt Betty: **"An open door may tempt a saint"**.

2. Sea of surprises
The hidden message is **"Seas are full of life too"**.

4. Pick the pair
The secret message is **"to each his own"**.
The objects that belong together are:

monkey	banana
dog	bone
William Tell	apple
Elvis Presley	hamburger
Charlie Chaplin	shoes
king	crown
4	missing from sum of 144
hat	feather
tooth fairy	tooth
Neptune	trident
Adam	fig leaf
caveman	club

5. Treacherous temple
The solution shows the path and the 14 eggs.

6. Letter litter
When the shapes are fitted together they spell out **"Burnt cat fears the fire"**.

7. Anna Gram Enterprises
The hidden word is **contaminated**.

8. Fragments from the Pharaohs

9. Forbidden colours
Here are the colour differences found on the first man.

11. Four-star puzzle
This solution is one of several possibilities.

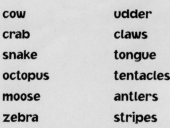

13. Which zoo?
The zoo is in **Paris**.

14. Step by step
The order for each hexagon:
A, bell, cloud, doll, elephant, frog, glass, house, ice cream, juggler, king, lemon, mouse, nest, octopus, pencil, question mark, rose, snail, tree, umbrella, violin, watch, xylophone, yacht, Z.

15. Magic word
The letters with the secret stamp spell out **please**.

16. What beast is that?
The animals' names and their body parts are:

ANIMAL	BODY PART
camel	humps
toucan	beak
elephant	ears
butterfly	antennae
pig	tail
rhinoceros	horn
cow	udder
crab	claws
snake	tongue
octopus	tentacles
moose	antlers
zebra	stripes

17. Disk dilemma

The image is a sea horse.

18. Age by age

The children's ages are:

Dora	15
Becka	8
Tim	7
Ruby	15
Karl	16
Tina	4

Rover, the dog, is four.

20. Astonishing anagrams

The inspirational sentence is:
"This is meant as incentive".

21. Opposites attract

Here are more opposites:

straight	bent
dirty	clean
white	black
dead	alive
long	short
fast	slow
wet	dry
round	square
tall	short
many	few
hot	cold
wide	narrow
full	empty
high	low

22. Restore the story

The film's title is **Robber**.

23. Pegs galore

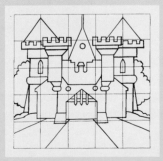

24. Where to?

The names of the cities are: **Melbourne, New York, London, Paris, Frankfurt, Tokyo**.

26. Slot in the slabs

You need the **top right slab** as the base for the **bottom left**.

27. Hexed paths

The solution shows the other possible paths, determined by the following:

Path 5   Animals that look backwards.
Path 6   Animals with red eyes.
Path 7   Blue backgrounds.
Path 8   Animals with blue eyes.
Path 9   Yellow background and blue animals.
Path 10 Frogs.
Path 11 Animals that are blue.

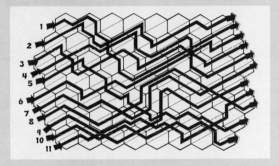

28. Find the city

The cities for each set of boxes are:
Madrid, Berlin, Ottawa, Dallas, Darwin.

29. Baffling balls

The two red balls are the odd ones out.

30. Mug shots

The mystery woman is:

31. Maths mystery

Whichever way you hold the paper, it adds up to **3608**.

32. Pick up sticks

The sticks spell out **Shakespeare**.

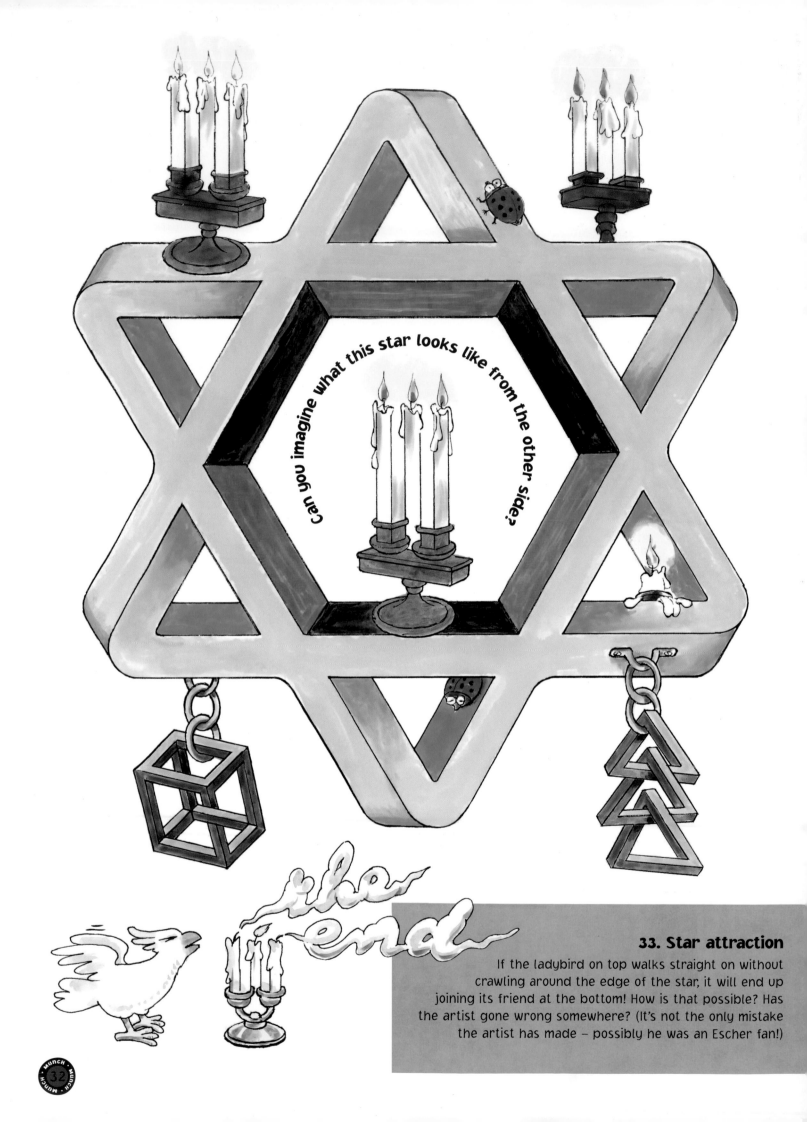

Can you imagine what this star looks like from the other side?

33. Star attraction

If the ladybird on top walks straight on without crawling around the edge of the star, it will end up joining its friend at the bottom! How is that possible? Has the artist gone wrong somewhere? (It's not the only mistake the artist has made – possibly he was an Escher fan!)